MIDNIGHT SKIES

EXMOOR IN VERSE

PUBLISHED BY

CHARMED HOLE
PUBLICATIONS

Edited and selected by

ATISHA McGREGOR AULD

First published in 2013 in the United Kingdom
by Charmed Hole Publications
Bank of Scotland, Kyle, Ross-shire IV40 8AB

ISBN 978 0 9522707 2 0

A CIP record for this book is available from the British Library

Produced in the West Country
Designed by Sue Snell, Totnes TQ9 5QR
Printed and bound by Brightsea Press Ltd, Exeter EX5 2UL

www.atisha.org.uk

Dedicated to

Hope L Bourne

1918-2010

Whose love for Exmoor was absolute

'Amen seven times over!'

'Amen seven times over!' is taken from *Wild Harvest* (1978) by Hope L Bourne

PREFACE

'MIDNIGHT SKIES – Exmoor in verse' is a twenty-first century tribute to Exmoor. A trio of hares guides us through the pages in the guise of a 'Muse' and gives us a glimpse of the beauty of the dark sky reserve.

My sincere thanks to all the poets who have contributed more than 8,000 words to this Exmoor poetry anthology proving that the written word is still, like music and art, held in high esteem – their poems will give strength to the moor.

Poet and reader are brought together by verse, with memories and visions giving us insight into the ancient power and mystery of Exmoor – encouraging us to stay vigilant in keeping the moor safe from modern day ills; impressing those officially responsible that there is a continuing need to protect and value the ethereal qualities, clear skies, archaeological sites, natural habitats, watercourses and wildlife.

Exmoor has attracted literati and royal patronage over the centuries and it is not difficult to imagine why people are drawn here to restore their well-being.

'May the soul of Exmoor survive and all those soles who walk on it continue to be inspired.'

Happy Reading . . .

Atisha McGregor Auld
November 2013 – Exmoor

Eclogue

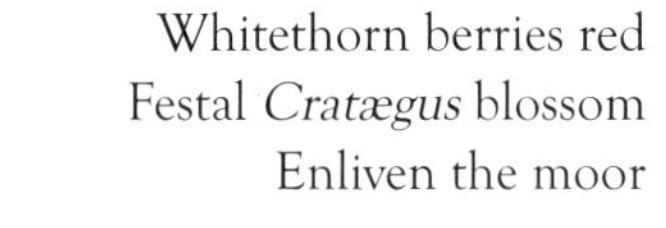

Whitethorn berries red
Festal *Cratægus* blossom
Enliven the moor

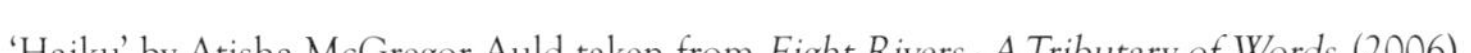

'Haiku' by Atisha McGregor Auld taken from *Eight Rivers - A Tributary of Words* (2006)

INTRODUCTION

Welcome to sixty Exmoor inspired poems: poems in every style – traditional, modern and contemporary. They come from local poets, and some from far away; from school children (some of their lines contributed through the innovative medium of digital imaging) to octogenarians; from well established poets and from poets previously unpublished – from almost every walk of life; from Exmoor people born and bred, and from others who have gravitated here more recently; from members of groups as well as from those who write by themselves, for pleasure, delight and often healing...

Recent research has confirmed the ability of poetry to trigger 'reappraisal mechanisms' which cause the reader to reflect and rethink their own experiences. Science is demonstrating that we are still only beginning to appreciate the wonderful powers of poetry.

Thank you to all the poets, and may these their poems give lasting pleasure.

Exmoor's International Dark Sky Reserve designation in 2011 has encouraged us to lift up our eyes to these hills in a spirit of hopefulness, and above and beyond them to the wonders of the firmament.

On Ferny Ball in an Autumn Storm was inspired by the pervading spirit in Exmoor of Hope Bourne, to whom this anthology is dedicated and, from whose philosophy we have much to learn.

Dr Richard Westcott
Poetry Co-ordinator and Adviser

ON FERNY BALL IN AN AUTUMN STORM

RHW (2011)

Bright beech branches wave in the wind
fragments flying. I turn from the west,
rain on my back, clothes tightly pressed.
Was that more green limbs flapping
or something different as if,
as if someone were striding
through the overgrown hedge?

Determined and purposeful, armed with a stick
the figure continues to vanish,
washed away in the rain with a wish
to be somewhere else. No shelter no company
available here. Just sharp surgings,
horizontal rain and prevailing gale,
such as she would know only too well.

Struck on the shoulder by a stick in the wind
I turn once again, feeling a summons,
I am part blinded and deafened
by elemental forces tearing at trees,
scattering unseen clouds. Nothing here
is tamed, for this is wildness where
the loose is freed and the free are caught.

Who would be out in a place like this
on a day such as this, unless flying
from home and some others, with a wish
to be absent? She's slipping past green trunks
of bent-over beech, whose branches wave
at a dwindling figure now blown away
by this westerly, and storm distorted senses.

Hope Bourne, writer and artist, lived by herself self-sufficiently in a caravan at Ferny Ball, a remote hill in Exmoor, for over twenty years. She died in 2010.

Requiem

FOR SEAMUS HEANEY

1939-2013

David Campbell

"*For the mountain grass*
Cannot but keep the form
Where the mountain hare has lain."

These, Seamus, are the words you whispered
Again and again in my ear
On the night of my fortieth birthday
Where they reverberate still.

And now you are laid under the grass
The imprint of the warm hare of your poetry
Keeps the form of not just your words
But of you.

Words whispered from *Memory* (1916) by WB Yeats 1865-1939

A BROWN HARE - Lepus europaeus 1

Stephen Lewis

I saw a lone Brown Hare
One of the wild unshod
Whose fleet feet kiss the sods
Runner for the joy of it
Patter cake boxer
Muse for myriad artworks
Its ink dipped charcoal tipped ears
Gave me the ancient archer's salute
It amber eyed me with a look I read as pity
For me whose toes never melt
The icing sugar early frost
Or crackle summer stubble
Always a barrier between
My sole and fecund earth
I hope your genes run on forever
I'll watch for them in Porlock Vale
Or Dunkery Hill
When it's cold enough
To see a hare's breath

AN EXMOOR ROMANCE

Yvonne Dale

When I was born I loved you
You could say I was born to love you
When I was a child how I loved to run around on you
You could say I gave you the run around
When I was a young adult how I loved to spend quality time with you
You could say the time I gave you was not quality
When I got married and moved away how I missed you
You could say our marriage was missing something
When I had my children I prayed they would understand your quiet beauty
You could say we never understood our children
When you left me I returned to the place I loved
You could say that your love was never returned
Oh how you make me Moor complete
You could say that now you are just an Ex

ANTLER MAN

Adrian Evans

Through tiny cobwebbed windows
I look
A lifetime of loving indulgence
The love of one man unravels
As my eyes take in the innumerable and ancient
Tools, benches and the ephemera made of red deer antlers
Everywhere walking sticks, candlesticks, chairs, key rings hang
Even a chair
Mixed with the silvery autumn Exmoor sun
The aura of the antler man is here
But this morning he is out shopping
With his wife
Memories of the timeless lives of the red deer of Exmoor
Grace his walls
Their majestic, primeval essence preserved
But for how long now this tiny shack?
        Memorial to the past,
                Gracing the present
                        Preserved for the future
Fortunate am I this morning to be standing on his floor, breathing his air, seeing what he sees
I will be back to take a small piece of this
Will he be there?

4

ARTISTIC FREEDOM

David Beanland

She tried to capture the moor, enclose it
in a painting, as others, once, had tried
to net the land with fields, those blank spaces
framed by banks of beech. Unlike them she chose it
not for gain, confinement, but for the wide
horizons a thoughtful soul embraces.

Distilling that immensity from paint
took years, and, as she aged, the barbs and banks
conspired to make it harder, but still she strove
to trap the grasses ruffled by a faint
wash of air, or sheep-scoured hedges where hanks
of wool trailed like the shifting clouds above.

Exmoor resisted her: its heathers brushed
aside the tints she tried and trees whose curve
had pencilled in the wind refused to yield
simply to her art. She learned at last to trust
those rarer moments when her skill would serve
the landscape and contrivance be concealed.

Years went by and what was once accessible
seemed hard to reach, barred by fields and fencing.
She felt the need to cut through such constraint.
I see her now, determined yet less able,
snipping at a snarl of wire and sensing
the freedoms of the moor, the freedoms of her paint.

N

AUTUMN'S STAG

Sophie Johnson

He prances across the moor,
Head held high.

Dappled brown,
Flecks of gold,
Amber eyes gleam,
Antlers, bare branches stretching to the sky.

He strides to the babbling brook,
Lowers his head,
And drinks.

He stands
Absorbing the last rays of sunlight
That flit through the trees.

Epitomising the beauty of his time.

BAMPFYLDE CLUMP - THE ROUND RING

Frances Presley

this turning turning of it
taken leaves
blown up
blown through

borne across
their talk
their saying
that they were saying

so many beech
blocked
beech clustered
dense but separate

fenced and speaking out
blowing out
circled round and back

taken over
offered levels
held forward branches
height above height
to overcome
to overreach

the pasture

N

BEAST

Patricia Millner

All that summer it prowled our dreams.
At first it was wary.
A townsman's dog might answer for
a lamb stripped to the bone.
But then the ewes...
From Molland Common
and Heasley Mill,
High Bray and Withypool
the daily death count grew.
It left its marks.
Ripped throats not like
the work of dogs.
Scats dark and twined with wool.
A clawless paw print by the stream.
Landrovers lurched across the moor,
farmers riding shotgun in the rear.
Big game trackers and the army came,
co-ordinating killings and reports
of eerie howls at dusk.
Their tripwire cameras spotted
only fox or deer.

To some it showed itself,
sometimes grey as granite,
sometimes brown,
a liquid presence fluently melding
into the shadow of a hedge
or slipping from the corner of the eye.
Or once to startled planners in a coach
who saw it lapping from a stream
but found their photos blank.
We joined the vigilantes,
searched our barns and linhays
for its daytime lair,
lamenting the slain sheep
and farmers' loss.
But deep in the dreams' maze
we willed it to survive
inhabiting the winding cleaves
ancient and untameable,
exacting its sacrificial due.

BREAK O - STONE FRAGMENT

Tilla Brading

break   O
pen

brake

beside the stones
break on the rocks

stone breaker
the rhythmic pound
ing   pound
ing   pound

chippings crunched
under the march
ing feet march
ing feet
'herpath'

line break
white space

never a white space in nature
lone stone in a windswept moor

teems buzzard circled
lark-staccato
kestrel eyeing
the hopping grasses

BROKEN DOWN

Noel Williams

The sky stops turning. All the stars stand still.
Alone, lost on the moor, my battery dead
midnight whispers all the tales I've read
of fey, black beasts, spirits that drink the will.
I've lost the path. My torch gives out. A mere
dark as seduction shimmers in the sedge.
The water beckons. I kneel at the edge,
hearing it sneer there's no way back from here.

Yet gorse has the scent of home, while the breeze
sings through cotton grass like a children's rhyme.
Faint light leafs the whitebeam and ash. And I'm
shouting, running to torches in the trees.
My hand wipes the wind's cold tears from my face.
The peat is not bitter or dark. It's soft as grace.

BURGUNDY CHAPEL

Giles Goodland

Brush the ferns aside and bow through an arch
where the moss steams. Wales fuzzes,
the stream's white noise shushes invisibly
on shingle and thistledown rises
like prayer. We had been watching clouds
make copies of themselves as brambles
lifted their berries to suckle on sun.

Priests beamed prayer from here, feeling for
a shine of deity, a clean world jumped
from mist. So if creation sings anywhere
it must be deep in this chantry's cistern,
among fern fiddleheads. It must hum in
seed-capsules, wing-cases, pollen, larvae
stirring under the wind, the thistle
clanking its faint armour under the sun.

Caterpillars eat windows. Imprisoned
in its cell a chlorophyll god
converts sunlight, and annually fails.
I had wanted to show you what had been
bigger in my past, those beaten walls,
the landslipped tongues caving to beach,
but it's as if there's been too much year:
the light around us decays and green's
inaudible engine has exhausted the sun.

Figure into the canvas this and more:
the dust and rusted dockseeds,
sky's tissues contracting around us,
the mud retracting, old man's beard
spent like semen across trees. Waiting
for wind's complications when listening to
that music it seems we could burn like
the fire itself. A butterfly opens its illumination
and nothing answers but language,
language rolling on its tongue the sun.

N

CHRISTENING

Elizabeth Bradshaw

A barren church. Bare stone walls, rigid pews.
The plants that grew either side of the altar
were faded frescos, past their prime.

My husband's large hand warming mine
as the Comfortable Words were recited.
And my time-share child. Did she cry?

I can't say. Searching heavenwards
beyond sneering gargoyles I'd found
the unexpected: a bat, spinning shadows

through the dusky winter daylight. The way
it rested on the arch of a stained-glass
window: a dark stain on pale stone.

A bat! All through the christening lunch
I replayed its crenelated flight, its teeth
spiked spindle sharp, our prayers

its harvest. Or gnats. Or not? Perhaps
it only flew because we had disturbed it?
A quiet cool retreat warmed by offerings

from ancient radiators, made noisy
by our incumbent praise. Oh God, perhaps
we were the death of it? Woken to find no food.

Starving. And me, worrying about this
on the dark drive home
because it's safer to fret over small things.

CHRISTMAS DAY AT RADDINGTON

Martin H Perry

The carol's faded: the chat's begun:
church door is opened: it's time to go:
beyond the exit, beneath the sun,
there glints and sparks, in the swelling snow,

pin-pricks of diamonds across the hill
in whiteness draped under pale blue sky,
thin hedge lines etched by a plume white quill,
while farmhouse, dark in its place close by,

a cake with icing by nature crimped,
as stolid trees, with their boughs bent low,
in static motion round meadows limped,
their wintry nakedness far from show:

though cold of frost with its silence sings,
no dance, no movement on arching hills
that stoop protective like angels' wings
as Christmas peace through the valley spills.

N

CROSSING-KEEPERS

Jane Mares

Across the moorland grasses
The pony herd came trekking,
Filing down through the heather
In line after their leader,

On neat, clattering hooves
They crossed the barren tarmac,
Foals at the mares' flanks
Dancing on dainty hoof-tips.

Heads up and ears forward,
Between the stilled traffic
They passed the gazing tourists
As once they passed bison, mammoths...

Custodians of the crossing-places,
Keepers of the ancient pathways –
Travel safely, little Exmoors,
On through many future centuries.

14

CULBONE STONE

Jay Ramsay

Three feet high in a glade of faery pines
grey and moss-covered – and lined
with an unmistakeable grin seen from the side
a Puckish Pan face in the permanence of stone
(to lighten up a dull day, who knows)
supplanted by a sign: gouged near the top
an encircled cross, lain like Jesus stumbling,
the long piece pointing down
from this high ground, to the hidden valley below

piercing its ear, and as your eyes re-align
it becomes a gravestone: but marking who, what, when?
A change as radical as it became betrayed
a ritual in the mists we can only imagine
become future, for us standing here now
in this extraordinary blue November morning
bent, tracing our fingers in its rain-smoothed shape,
for our own journey of remembering

under the world, and out of time.

N

EXE VALLEY

Mary Foxwood (née Reece)

I can hear the river rushing, rushing onward through the night.
I can see the silver moonbeams touching all with ghostly light,
Though now the mist is slowly rising, wreathing everything from sight.

Far away and in the distance comes the barn owl's mournful cry
Through the stillness of the night – beware oh mouse that's doomed to die!
Night will shield you from most terrors, but not this hunter's piercing eye.

EXILE

Sarah Westcott

The year the quince swelled, swifts dipped
over our city garden,
and the blue sky opened up for us all –
we saw so clearly the children
and felt in our hearts the child's clear song,
bones lengthening, heads full of light
as rhubarb turned to the sun, pinkening
and little sandals lost long ago were warm.

Let us go back to the moors,
deep coombes where larks ring up their truth
and scatter ribboned notes that fall
like strands of soft-brushed hair,
where the sessile oaks, standing stones
and hanging trout know all that we forget –
far from the wilderness, wide skies
until the swifts reclaim us.

EXMOOR

Anthony Watts

– flayed to the bone with wind and rain,
where watercourses double as rights of way
and the black-nibbed sheep
are tireless scribes
who annotate an endless text of grass

– where we came upon a massive oak,
uprooted, upended, having dragged
from the underworld
a half-ton boulder, which it held
aloft in its claws like a trophy

– where the river trots
on small white hooves
over the pebbles or – slowing – spreads
l u m i n o u s
over treacle-pot depths

and the mist, like a night nurse,
comes with soothing hands
to the long dormitories of the hills.

EXMOOR ALIEN

Marion Elmes

The Chains cut across clear cobalt
Breath catches at space and silence.

Pair by pair
Horns appear over the ridge
Elongating out from under ginger curls.
Pop-eyes bulge and glint.
Shaggy, still, burnt-orange bodies multiply,
Stump legs fat at knees. Bloated bellies.
Eyes watch. Wait…

Are they creeping nearer?
Run! Stop! Which way?
Featureless grasslands abound now.
Wire reeds snatch at calves –
Boots squelch in belching bog edge –
Mud flies leech onto cheeks
And suck.

Swipe!
The wipe smears scarlet.

Metallic rasps above from black
Bone-picking birds

Circling
Laughing.

EXMOOR'S SUMMER REACH

Miranda Cox

I would explore your lichen ways
your river reach and hill stretch
as you birth the sun into lightfoot days

puzzles of beaten heather
scratch the nose of a moorland mare
as she learns your rough terrain

you call across restless skies
ponder at stone-cool bridges
and unravel cliffs to the cry of spray

watch impassive the hunt and scream
the kill of fox and stag, pound of paw
dull on dust, as hounds pant into their dream

villages scrum down in your shade
at Dunkery Beacon your body drops
like bleached ribs into valley fold

you lilt through a twist of oak
patched with moss and bewitch me
from the toll of sap-drained moods

I am dusk and star on your moonlit moor
held in the dark of an otter's swim
still in your long night breath
till the soft-lipped touch of dawn

FMD IN THE WINGS

James Crowden

Every morning they sniffed the wind
And looked south.
They were nervous, on the moor,
Any vehicle was viewed with suspicion.

Rumours were rife of golden handkerchiefs
Men moving stock late at night
Bed and breakfast sheep
Playing away from home.
The borrowed trailer
Squeaking its way down narrow lanes.

Every outbreak pinned on a map
Like guerrilla raids, one here one there,
Then doubling back, grasping at straws,
The uncertainty of dark shadows.
Scanning the horizon with binoculars.
The distinctive smell of pyres and burnt flesh
Plumes that ran northwards.

As each farm was taken out
The air became tinged
Sleepers and disinfectant in short supply.
Diggers and sedatives on standby
Shotguns loaded, barricades manned
Rendezvous points tagged and taped.

Exmoor held its breath and waited.

FINISHING THE HEDGING

Richard Westcott

He leans on the branch and taps the bent wood –
skin crinkles. His blade slides inside
the stick splits.
This hazel lies flat now a new horizontal
joining the others to follow uphill.

He transfers some weight, shifting position
his foot finds a space in the basket work
twigs and stumps.
The new strand is bundled up, under and over
joining the others to follow uphill.

He straightens to stand and surveys his work –
new wood revealed, curved parallel rods
tense and straight
ready to spring upwards later. He jumps down
joining the others to follow uphill.

FROM ROBOROUGH CASTLE TO THE HOAR OAK TREE

Patricia Glover

At the end of the lane I know the stream
With stepping stones and a rope to steady.
Hoar Oak Water where we swam with fishes,
Swung dizzy from trees, fell laughing in reeds,
Where our campfire stories sparked shocked delight
And savages with sticks was just a game;
Where we searched the sedge for the treacherous
Sundew, watched aghast its innocent prey,
Scared safe in those long summer days.

Today the sky is racing, crowded.
I go to search beyond the stile
And pick a pathless course.
Past the wiry blackthorn,
Unmoored, I search a way
To where the valley empties
And barely tinted ochre banks
Shoulder land that's hard and spare
And there's the single Hoar Oak Tree.
No grand or lofty oak tree this
But there and standing, still

It seems a place to sit a while.
Then, tethered by my memories,
I'll step my own tracks back.

N

GATHERING SHEEP

Molly Goodland

They rode out before sunrise, their dogs
nosing the ground close behind as if
a clue to the day might be found there.

Once they hit the moor setting the horses
to a good gallop down to the pens.

Other commoners, already there, checking
the hurdles, greeting them with "What time
of day d'you call this then?" and "Always
late you two!" the pattern of their days set
in generations, as laired as their sheep
are laired to their own particular stretch
of the common.

They all ride out over the miles of moor,
the sun now up, licking with gold and
shadow secret hollows where sheep might lie.

In coombes where the dogs stop to drink,
lambs panic and run to mothers whose slow
memories stir, but there is no time so they
run each to each for the comfort of numbers.

Tirelessly the dogs circle and fetch from
different stretches of the moor, bringing
sheep together, shepherding them back
to the pens where the old man and the boy (as if
a year had not passed) still wait.

Under the hedge, in the shade of the trees
the horses droop and swish their tails
while the dogs rest, one eye open, tired
and without malice, waiting for their own sheep
unpenned, and for the shout and the whistle
and the long slow journey back to the farm.

HARES ON A MARCH MORNING

Di Cater

In this early light, diffused by a cobwebby mist,
They are at first invisible.
But wait. Be still. They are here –
Subtly camouflaged against the moorland scrub,
Poised for flight or boisterous play.
They are by turns both clumsy and elegant,
With their lean frames and those huge hind feet.
The wide-angled placement of dark-lashed eyes
Affords a panoramic view with barely a swivel
Of a whiskery head, ears a-twitch.
The embodiment of vigilance, they sense a presence
As the March wind whips the sheltering grasses –
And they're off: a cavorting trio, dancers, not quite balletic,
Bordering upon the manic in their bravura.
Sure of outrunning any predator, they own their space.
Savour this privileged sighting: put away the camera.
Use only your eyes, then leave, quietly.

HAWKCOMBE - 19TH OCTOBER

Stephen Carroll

Descending the hill path, unthinking,
I dropped into the cackle and riot of rooks
circling below me in the oak wood.
When I'd walked that quarter mile
they'd gone, with all their racketing,
leaving a place of silence, framed
by hurrying sky above and rushing stream below,
and a young jay dead on the ground
beside me, its downy breast
still warm, its body gorgeous
and unmarked save for a neat
gimlet hole behind the lolling head.
I pulled a dazzling feather from the wing
to keep (it fell out later on the train),
and went my way, leaving the body
to be stripped of glory like a god,
dead on the field of battle at the close of day.

HEAVEN ON EARTH

Doris Sloley

I've heard it said that heaven is what
You want it most to be,
So I shall make a list of all
The things I'd like to see.

Lace cobwebs on the meadow grass,
Some bright September morn;
A blackbird, sweetly singing in
A field of waving corn.

A river I can walk beside
With fish that jump and play,
And stepping stones that I can cross
Upon a summer's day.

I'd have my gentle collie dog
And sheep with lambs, newborn.
Some ponies with rough, shaggy coats,
Returning home at dawn.

There would be hills and valleys and
A road down to the sea.
The people I have loved the best
Would all be there with me.

But I've no need to make a list
Of treasures fine and rare.
Just let heaven mirror Exmoor
And I'll be happy there.

JANUARY TREES

Virginia Hobart

Now ghostly behind, then sharply defined
against the morning mist
with the switched-on clarity of an X-ray screen:
limbs lovely like bones
revealing shape and structure,
health and strength, injury and age:
gnarled and knuckle-fingered oak,
outstretched open-handed ash,
doomed once high-and-mighty elm,
steadfast sheltering sycamore,
pliant willow, graceful birch,
wind-whipped, crippled hill-top thorn:
all bare in the turning year
and black against the morning mist,
more clearly seen than in their summer green.

JOURNEY OF THE SALMON

Jenny Lewis

Pierced – side open, bleeding
On this journey
Back to your source
  Womb of creation
    Water flowing
      Pounding the depths
As you leap.

For as the river flows
It meets – time and again
That moment of decision –
A brief moment of hesitation:
Which eddy will I follow –
The fast flowing turbulent
Leap over the boulder –
Or lie at rest in a deep pool
Awaiting my destiny?

LAST SUPPER

Rosemary Burnett

She is startled by her dexterity
with the honed hunting knife,
the skinning completed in a trice.
'Poor hare', the child murmurs.

Gingerly manoeuvring
the swill bucket with her feet,
she closes her eyes against
the sight of the paunching,
tugging still-warm entrails,
letting them slither
into the pulsating waste.

A burly figure blocks
the light in the doorway.
He scrapes the chair,
takes his special place
at the farmhouse table,
drums his impatience,
then champs without finesse.
The child does likewise.
Neither notices the gravy
congealing on her plate.

LYNMOUTH DISASTER

Mark Haworth-Booth

He saw a black cloud creeping from the West,
edged with purple and deep red,
while another darker band
sped underneath it from the East.

He saw the clouds burst open and deliver
five inches in one hour,
tearing away the moorland cover,
hurling everything into the rivers,

sweeping the cattle off their feet,
with poultry, foxes, deer and horses,
then motor cycles, vans and cars,
rushing and smashing out of the night,

uprooting trees and rolling boulders
through sheets and jags of lightning,
battering bridges and bankside buildings –
the Lyn rivers roaring, house-high monsters.

He saw a drenched policeman in a phone box,
trying to call for help
from Ilfracombe and Barnstaple.
He saw him suffering electric shocks.

He saw cars gliding downhill to the harbour,
continuing silently into the brine –
headlights submerged and green –
their circuits shorted by the rising water.

He saw a whole hamlet swept out to sea –
ten cottages with their foundations –
leaving well-kept hill-side gardens
and a child's bedstead nesting in a tree.

He heard of a dish of eggs, and not one broken,
in a house razed to the ground.
He heard that under a butcher's slab they found
a nine year old named Kenneth Bowen.

The stranger learns from Lynmouth that wild nature
tears masonry and innocence like paper.

N

MISSING FROM EXMOOR

Catherine Nicholls

Why wasn't I consulted before they left?
I am angry,
Somewhat bewildered,
Sad.
The swifts left Exmoor
(Or at least Winsford
Suddenly
For ever?)
Over which they mastered the summer skies,
Shrieking,
Keening,
Impossible to ignore;
Gone without telling, without explaining.
Gone too are the house martins,
Chatting from under my eaves,
Leaving without my wishing them farewell,
Their desiccated cob nests
Bursting with allegedly endangered sparrows.
The swallows,
Though much diminished in number,
Bless them,
Are breeding.
I leave the barn door
Propped open with an old broken thumbstick,
Listening for their offspring.
I look up into the
Intense cerulean pink-streaked longest day's twilight
And grieve.
Are they there?
I must have an eye test.

MOON OVER ST LUKE'S

Saffron Summerfield

Slipping quietly out of St Luke's
into a night still fused with light
moon full to bursting
air rich with the scent of ramsons
I sense I've entered another land
not strange or foreboding
more an unexplored friend

This 'newness of place'
wild and familiar
touches deep a hidden coil
memories dormant slowly unfurl
the smell of burnt earth
reveals a yearning
to renew old ways

I walk home slowly
mindful of Hope Bourne's story
her creative freedom casts a spell
pastel images of untamed land
sweet with heather and gorsey dew
blood on the grass
hounds on the hill

I wend my way along a hollow lane
deep in the shadow of ancient hills
water trickling through stone and clay
beguiling and constant
like a long lost friend
I walk and walk
till night becomes day

NATURE'S SILENCE

Ruby Winzer

She listens, a dark sheet, no volume
Hills stifle at the utter dread of it
The river weeps sadly

No sound
Days slowly pass
Summer, Autumn, Winter

But as Spring bursts through...
Crack, cheep, footsteps
Spring has broken the silence spell

New life has sprouted
New noise
And a colossal bleat of volume.

NEW YEAR

Slowly the silent embrace captures
The natural wildness of the open space
Frosted fingers whiten as they freeze
And linger
At the dawn
And the breaking of the day

Undulations of the meadow and moor
Disappear in the shrouding mists
Of the cold grey as they embrace as before
And permeate and creep in dell and hollow
Seeping as it is creeping
Stealing the hedgerows and distant hills and
valleys of the Doones
Shrinking life into itself under the stiffened cold
As if to swallow
Hiding with frosted breath and
Silver and white glistening.

The ridged hardened earth is unforgiving
In the foggy grey mass; brushed white with frost
The dry ice stays sharp and splintering
In pot holes and trodden tracks
That holds fast the crooked trees
Bent in time in wizened winds
Distorted from the twisting tips
To the frozen sprawling roots

The weather wise sheep press tight
Into hidden hollows
As the day lengthens
The cold grey day of bitter winds and leaden sky
The blue hued coldness that lies over the hills
Cheerless, eerie
No noonday brightness
The frosted fingers stay frozen
White, bright, glistening amid the grey
Enhanced with a magic
That surrounds still statuesque trees.

NEW YEAR

Vicki Lowen

Rural cottages stand with large laden log piles
By the broken saw bench sheds
Prepared, shuttered,
Just the starlings dive and sweep
Low over the hedges in huge flocks
Or rise amazingly from frozen grass
With the noise of a thunderclap
Awakening the day for a moment
Then passes into the grey frozen stillness.

As the short day closes
The silent moor captures the scene
There is an emptiness about the cold
Like a void of un-captivated space
Shielding the valleys and the hills
Making them never quite accessible
Distant, ethereal
Far away the eyes of a car on the distant road
Forms, momentarily, a glow of light in the gloom
The short day is gone as the desolation of the
dusk settles
And a blackness pushes the speed of the twilight
And the night begins as we seek the moon
With thoughts of home and expectations of
a New Year.

NOVEMBER EVENING

Rosina Winiarski

The journey home was delayed
by a flock of sheep moving
at a leisurely pace along the road.
They snatched at mouthfuls of grass
and spilled into gateways
but there was nowhere to hide
and they were driven forwards
by the small, prick-eared collie
weaving tirelessly from side to side.
The sky was changing from a colourful
mise-en-scène of pinks, blues and greys
to a spread of low-lying clouds
streaked with the rays of the setting sun.
And as the sheep disappeared over the brow
of the hill the afternoon became evening
and a bird flew towards a gossamer moon.

OCTOBER AIR

Audrey Coldrick

Hear the song of autumn
lilting through the trees
with hum and strum of
lissom limbs swaying in
the breeze.

Like maestro plucking violin
in haunting melody
nature's chanter rises in
plaintive rhapsody, punctuated
by the bleat of birds upon the wing
in rhythmic orchestration to the tune
that autumn sings.

ON DUNKERY BEACON

Jenny Gibson

I yielded to temptation
and climbed to the top of the hill,
despite the fact that it was a
sweltering, sunny, summer Sunday
and Exmoor's highest point was
sure to be thronged with people.

Yet, when I reached the top,
it was eerily empty,
and the view devoid of life,
except for a scattering of sheep,
a dappling of deer
and the bawling of bullocks.

This was what I had dreamed of,
back in my previous city-bound existence:
high hills, big skies
and blessed space simply to be.

Eventually, the penny dropped.
West Somerset was all indoors,
Behind drawn curtains, watching England
lose the World Cup.

N

ON PORLOCK HILL - DAYBREAK

Eric Mayo

High, up to the summit, climbing;
No more new, unknown, beguiling
Pathways through the woodlands, turning,
Twisting, dark and secret ways.
Here the track runs steep but wending
Gently, wide and open – smiling.

From the shadows to the brightening
Moorlands in their new awakening,
My heroic, hard won, freedom
Brings me, weary and alone,
To a dawn-lit ancient kingdom,
To this place of fractured stone;
Of yellow gorse and purple heather;
Wind and space and fickle weather;
Misty summits, far off, waiting,
All beneath a broad sky vaulting.

No human eye can view its ending
Nor contain this wild perfection.
No artist's brush nor camera's action
Truly holds, in reproduction,
This vast accomplishment of Nature.
Then all around, both far and near
Comes light; sacred, bright, reviving
Light and golden glory, rising.

PATIENCE

David Spark

A boy of ten waits in his wartime home
whilst others, thought as men,
take the ashes through the Lenten rain.

The cars are black on this and every day;
he places a red nine on a black ten
and looks towards the garden gate again.

They slowly drive in petrol-rationed way;
only his mother turning to look back;
he moves the ten to the adjacent jack.

Across the now shelled moor they come to Oare;
the boy no longer sees the fallen card
but stares again across the windswept yard.

They throw his father round a stunted thorn
and turn towards the boy who waits at home,
knowing not how deep the grief has grown
that he the younger son was left at home.

POINT OF VIEW - R ponticum

Janice Cockett

Down the dell they riot,
a profusion of saris, swirling
like nautch girls to titillate
this hoary raja, lichened,
eroded furrows cleaving
his brow.

Imperial purple, they taunt
the polite, understated
sky, so fond of grey.
Permian sandstone red as
hart's blood, red as sunset in
arctic climes, he wore their
colour once.

The glaciers barely touched
him – his furrows marks of
grace, not livid scars gouged
from tortured rock, yet still
he aged, rhododendron purple
leeched to mist of heather,
magnolia petals warm
as sun-kissed skin
a memory.

At dawn they start, the
National Trust volunteers,
war declared on this
ineradicable weed. The
raja sighs, blinks back
a tear, relapses
into dreams.

QR CODE POEMS - THE COLERIDGE WAY

Dunster, Nether Stowey and Porlock First Schools

As I travel down the path, I stumble, trip and laugh,
as bouncy grass gives way to my boots when I tread.

I could hear grass waving below my feet and the small
tall birds above, in the air, singing all around me.
And when they stopped I scarce heard the air
whispering and then, just then, I stumbled across
Conygar Tower.

I saw branches like octopus tentacles grasping on to
small twigs.
Ivy dripping down from the arch like a waterfall!
Branches swooping like witches' fingers.

I saw a buzzard flying in the air up above me brushing
through the trees.
My fingers started to shiver in the breeze and the
ravens in the trees started to sleep.

Dawdling coldly on the stony path, the smell of the
gorse bush, pitter-patter rain hush rain hush.
I could taste the imaginary icicles on my tongue being
created by the cold air.

I picked up a freezing rough stone.

I could taste the bitter wind rushing left and right.
The sweet smell of the wild garlic.
I heard the gentle stream trickling across the stones.
I felt the thin veins of a lime coloured leaf.
I heard the shaky rattle of horses' reins.

At Webbers Post I saw the raindrops chill down the
shelter, the fog looked like a silver wolf.

Relentless fog and rain drawing shimmering colour
from the day.

N

Co-ordinator Christopher Jelley

SHE IS EXMOOR

Jenny Daisley

She is there
centuries reincarnating
ageless and youthful
changeless and static
shifting and moving
minute by year
weathered and worn
pristine and fresh.

I journey home.
She is there.
In the distance
bright and pretty
wonderfully verdant
lacking sophistication
set off by azure skies
sunbeam bright
dark and choleric
behind swirling veil
or with white epaulettes
standing out on guard
while others sleep or did not
venture in arctic darkness
aloof, emotionless, frosty.
She is there.

I will go soon
leaving unfathomed
the mystery she is
savour my imaginings.
Farewell to the creatures
she is sustaining there –
the myriad of deer, pony,
dormouse, grey squirrel...
silver-washed fritillary,
holly blue, purple hairstreak,
Dartford warbler,
pied flycatcher, redstart,
woodpecker, nuthatch,
buzzard, dipper,
goosander, guillemot,
razorbill, kittiwake,
magnificent peregrine falcons.

Farewell cotton grasses,
heathers, bog mosses,
favourite gorse, whortleberry,
cranberry, crowberry,
the ivy-leaved bellflower,
bog asphodel – no Hades here.
They are there now.
She is there.

SINCE DOOMSDAY...

Caroline Carver

goats huh!
billy goats gruff on the moor
dancing in and out
of the Valley of the Rocks

slayers of demons
snorters of fearsome reputation
forecasters of weather
banishers of evil spirits

let's set our horns to that fat sheep
send him over the cliff!
watch his body bounce on the way down
like a white balloon

let's lean over the fence
in our warm waterproof overcoats
eat winter flowers
chew the cud – sleep again

on days of mischief
we rut on the cricket-pitch
stare at visitors
with basilisk eyes

but it is our way, you know –
to our friends we are charming
our kids dance like young fauns
on the rock terraces

SNOWDROP VALLEY

The season is upon us, it is that time of year,
Like a magnet tugging at my heart, Snowdrop Valley lures me near.
Miss a year? Why not?
I say. There are other sights to visit, spread your wings,
An inner voice whispers, new horizons beckon you. But yet,
Miss a year? I cannot.

Ready to go: boots, coat, hat, scarf, camera, all is here.
I feel the joy already, the thrill like every year.
Miss a year? Why not?...
Who knows? Next year I may not be able to go
An extra busy month will come, there may be too much snow.
Miss a year? I cannot.

We're almost there, just up the hill and park,
Don our gear and ponder routes, which choice is right this year?
Miss a year? Why not? Never.
Oh the joy of setting off, through Cutcombe, down the lane,
We see snowdrops now, a few at first, a gentle overture.
Miss a year? I cannot.

SNOWDROP VALLEY

Jacqueline Patten

Across the field, the steep decline down to the bridge,
The glow I feel, more buds appear. So pleased to say
I did not, Miss this year.
Along the river banks, more snowdrops every year, and...
We've some way to go before the valley will appear.
Miss a year? I cannot.

We're there... my soul sings out...

The magic of your carpet appearing every year,
It thrills my eyes in many ways like music does my ear.
Miss this year? Why not?
But I cannot Miss a year, I find, in case, well, just in case
The spell you cast twelve months ago has lost some of its grace.
Miss this year? I cannot.

We're there. The crowds, the bus, the shared delight,
The way the sun filters through, with perfect rays of light.
Miss a year? I could not.
We enter, lost in the world I conjure up at night,
The memory of this diamond gem, remains within my sight.
Miss a year? I cannot.

STEPPING OUT ON EXMOOR

Alison Tanton

On the edge of an August evening
Stepping out from the constant clamouring –
Away from the woes of the world.
Here where white ribbon clouds unfurl
Above the fine curves of the hills,
Such balm to man's modern ills.
Bees give voice to the silence
Lulling all thoughts to abeyance.
This place everchanging, yet always the same:
Unbroken, protected, beloved.

THE BALLAD OF CROYDON HILL

Sarah Doyle

When howls abound on Croydon Hill, to echo through the moors,
we tell ourselves it's just the wind – but dead-lock all our doors.

For though our rationale insists it's no more than a breeze,
imagination takes us back to bygone centuries…

and when a Croydon ploughboy came to Rodhuish, and stayed
until the village Smithy there had fixed his broken blade.

The locals entertained him to a terrifying thrill –
the story of a devil said to haunt the local hill.

That night, the japing butcher's boy then hid himself within
the horned head of a bull, to scare his friend out of his skin.

Across the dark and gloomy moor the Croydon lad made tracks;
the butcher's boy jumped out to feign those devilish attacks.

The ploughboy fought back with his blade, not knowing of the jape,
and scarpered home, across the hill, with tales of his escape.

Next day, a bull's head, stained with blood, was found, but not the lad.
The butcher's boy was missing, with no sighting to be had.

Folks said the Croydon Devil's hand had snatched him clean away,
and many claim his spirit haunts the moors until this day.

So next time you hear ghostly howls that whisper through the trees,
lock all your doors and windows, then pray God it's just the breeze.

N

THE FAIRY GLEN

David T Hawkings

As I descended down the hill
And entered in the copse
I found a clearing 'twixt the trees
Carpeted with velvet moss.

And in the centre on the ground
A trodden track was marked;
It circled round an oaken stump.
The sun was shaded dark.

I closed my eyes to dream again;
The fairies came in view,
They danced around the fallen tree
Splashing in the dew.

Skipping round and round they went,
All linked their tiny hands
And from a nearby covert came
A tiny silver band.

A drum it boomed with rapid beat
The trumpets trilled a call;
A violin began to play;
Sweet music one and all.

Then I awoke from dreaming there
Expecting all had gone,
But no! the fairies still remained
Their instruments brightly shone.

Twas not a dream but real life
My tiny pixie men;
I see them now each time I go
Into their secret glen.

THE GREY MARE - THE DANCER

Kathleen Moore

The grey mare stood
Elegant and alone on the crest of the hill
Gazing all around her, ever alert and so very still
Morning had just broken, she felt so alive.

New dawn arriving, red hues, scudding white clouds
Fast changing the sky.

She focused her gaze upwards and stretched
Her legs growing longer her body so light
Her grey coat now glorious, bright silvery white
As she paused again softly
Her thoughts preparing to fly
Just one more glance backwards
At all that she had left.

She knew her way onwards was calling her fast
She wanted to go now
It was time and she was ready.
She felt her light softening now
As her tired eyes closed
And she knew she should leave.

She thought of her friends, just a few left now
Others to meet again soon
Her ears twitched in anticipation
She whinnied with excitement
Her body tensed with sensation
As she hovered a moment
Waiting to fly
She slipped out of her old skin
And to her full height
As she turned towards sunrise

Legs like a dancer, higher and higher
She extended herself fully to the light in the sky
As she turned away gracefully
And her spirit took flight.

THE HERON

Rosemary Toeman

The seaward side of the bridge
He stands.
Steady, eye gleaming.

Riveting the stream
He stands
Waiting, eye ready.

A girl. A dog. On the bridge.
He checks
Stiffening, eye turning.

Wings wide, statesmanlike, austere
He lifts.
One effortful swing

Above water, willow, pine
He steers.
Beating, reeling, up.

A chevron riding the cloud,
He leaves.

THE LEK

Joyce Jones

There, just to the west of Molland Moor Gate
I saw Blackcock at their display.
The grassy space
With cocks abound,
In pairs the males contested for a mate,
With plumage ruffled for the fray,
So beak to face
They sparred around,
Their black wings held out and white
tails a-fanned,
Each cock came at other in battle grand.

On moor, with heather sprouting to the sky,
Waltzed each cock, with lyre tail held proud,
That trampled patch
Was circled round
With many modest greyhens, peeping, shy,
That took no part, but stood in crowd
Watching the match
From side of ground,
For their lord's choice, they docilely waited,
When with winning birds they would be mated.

The Exmoor grouse, for ever in that way,
In Spring had used that self-same place:
The age-old ring
Was hallowed ground,
Where Blackcock had carried out their display;
But it's no longer their own base,
Just purple ling
Now grows around,
The birds have failed to breed and thrive.
What plight!
So it's fifty years since I saw that sight.

THE LIFE ON EXMOOR

The golden Gorse, and a girl on a horse, with a dog, of course, on Exmoor.
And the game and the gun, and the Fox on the run, "in season" for some, on Exmoor

The Farmer follows his furry flock, and the barmaid watches the tavern clock,
on Exmoor
The painter with her board and oils, struggling with the colour of soils, on Exmoor

Love to walk amongst the Heather, keeping one eye on the weather, it changes fast,
on Exmoor
Four foot of snow and there's nowhere to go, unless you're a crow, on Exmoor

And the huntsman in Pink, thinks the 'antis' all stink, it's life on the brink, on Exmoor
The poacher works with snare and gun, the 'Coppers' will have him on the run,
on Exmoor

And the Rambler studies his dog-eared map, while his dog lays down for a well-earned
nap, on Exmoor
Go and visit our reservoirs, you could learn to sail in a couple of hours, on Exmoor

The rough looking Pony who is never lonely, with more of its kind, on Exmoor
The wild rolling hills and hidden mills, and the views that thrill, on Exmoor

THE LIFE ON EXMOOR

(John Stenner)

A herd of Deer grazes on a hill, and never ceases to give a thrill, so hard to see when they all stand still, on Exmoor
A Fox's brush makes a Chicken rush, there's a panic, and crush, as his red jaws, munch... to death, on Exmoor

Ancient woodlands clad the Cleves, and nourish the ground with fallen leaves, on Exmoor
Old oaks wrapped in history, keep their secret mystery, and all they've seen... and yet to see, on Exmoor

Rivers run with fattened trout that poachers like to tickle and clout, or simply fish, to get them out, on Exmoor
Search in fields for Fairy Rings, go early day as the birds all sing, and fill your bags with mushrooms' bling, on Exmoor

Birds of prey on hollow wings, looking down for furry things... to eat, on Exmoor
A Jet flies over fast and low, and here he comes, and there he goes, on Exmoor

The North Devon link and brakes that stink, bringing girls who wink, on Exmoor
The cold second home of a banking gnome, who comes down to roam, on Exmoor

THE LIFE ON EXMOOR

John Stenner

The sky at night, with her stars so bright, is a humbling sight, on Exmoor
Grey mists hang like hanks of cotton, on a ruined village, long forgotten, on Exmoor

See the folk in the village shop, where people stop, to know what's what, on Exmoor
Lovers hold hands, making Rose-tinted plans, as the Sun goes down, on Exmoor

Churchyards cradle the long passed souls, which have lived their lives, and found their goals, on Exmoor
And the calves and the lambs, and the foals and fawns, that the farmers shall all.... hope, to be born.... on Exmoor.

THE NEW BOY IN TOWN

Austin L Brownrigg

He'd come from 'up north' had this bit of a lad,
By way of a varied and well-travelled path,
To take up residence in pastures anew,
Down there in Somerset, all wet with the dew.

He settled in Dulverton, God only knows why,
There's nowt there, in fact, most folks drive by.
But if you care to stop and take a look,
It's like opening up a very old book.

Aye, the buildings are old, 'n some's looking tired,
But it's the people who make it. They are inspired!
They'll wish you "Good Day", and mean
what they say,
And to help and advise they'll go out of their way.

"That job you wants doin' – 'twill be done directly".
Could mean tomorrow or next Pancake Tuesday.
Oh, it will get done of that have no fear,
And at the end of the day it won't cost too dear.

The answer in fact is of time to lose track,
Just set your clock in local time, and sit back,
Just smile, be happy, wish folk a "Good Day",
And the worry of a heart attack will just fade away.

THE RACE

Susan J May

I raced across the tarmac road,
I've done it once before,
I started out at half past three
And got there ten to four.

I'm just a hairy biker,
Without a bike you see,
So travelling takes me quite some time,
A caterpillar me!

I have to dodge the traffic
Or I end up squashed and flat.
Lunch for p'raps some hungry bird
I just don't fancy that!

In wait till nearly half past three
Before the kids leave school
And then I start my daring race –
To wait I'd be a fool.

Why go at all – you might well ask,
I might not go again,
But life is good the other side
Oh... here comes the rain.

THE UNIVERSE - DARK SKY ON EXMOOR

Jillian Merer

A surprise in a dark sky
The brightness of stars
The birth of creation
Amazing light from a million years.

A black cloak pierced by
shiny points of light.
Daytime noises abate
for the heavens are singing.

A night time rendezvous
The vastness is humbling
and we, a tiny speck
in this awesome universe.

THERE'S A PLACE IN THE WEST

David Firman

There's a place in the west
Where narrow rivers flow
Over boulder and rock
To the sea far below.

Where plump salmon leap
On their migratory run
And diamond glints sparkle
In the late autumn sun.

WATERSMEET

Cristina Navazo-Eguía Newton

We are of one mind to follow the water
down the coombe, where it runs white and
loud enough
to keep us quiet, so our thoughts, unheard,

draw in like stalked deer into the recess
of the woods, losing their thread through the
whitebeam trees.
Though we tread on the windfall

of their white-backed leaves
and their spent roses mouldering into
unsweetened soil,
our senses hang with the clustered fruits,

the all-out stake of their invested strength,
not yet red from the sun's stints or bletted mellow
by the frosts,
an ambush of hope in a trail of shortcomings,

like an ore of iron dreamed of at the end
of a shaft, quicklime smouldering in the belly
of the kiln,
charcoal loaded with heat to smelt the past:

all bitter stuffs that gall before they're ripe.
We are ready for this. Outside the dead mine's mouth,
we stop
and take in the spore-blistered undersides

of ferns growing from the wounds of earth,
the woodruff's syrup scent, the bilberries' black
acid hearts,
the stones, moss-mummed, and stock-still.

And hear the East Lyn's waters roughing against
the Hoar Oak's.

WINTER SKY

Such words that travel from the heart
to strike a chord
yet stand apart

such words that say the sky is blue
the winter sun
in hazy view

But I have tarried far too long
and winter's beast
has grown too strong

it freezes limbs and lives are lost
while wrapping beauty
in its frost

It chills the blood and gnaws the bones
discarding life
so briefly known

I sit beneath the winter sky
and hours are spent
on asking why

asking why the snow must fall
or why my dreams
still grow so tall

O shadowless the silver moon,
too bright the sky
with winter's tune

The leaves that bore their days so well
have added to
the sombre spell

So sharp the mirror from above,
so huge the sky
to fill with love

and tiny birds with frozen wings
can't beat the air
or softly sing

WINTER SKY

Richard Spiers

The winter beast has shown its claws
and words are clenched
in frozen jaws

how tight the lip and tight the heart
when autumn fades
and winter starts

As winter grips and strips us bare
we turn to fire
and comfort there

dreams are cast within the flame
and eyes will seek
the wind to blame

O holy flame
O blood of life
tame the beast to end this strife

melt the cold upon the fire
and claim the beast
of winter's mire

INDEX OF POETS & Contents

END NOTES

A BROWN HARE - *Lepus europaeus* 1
Is the largest of the British hares – known to be present in the UK, 2,000 years ago and now rarely seen.
Its black-tipped ears, approximately four inches long, are symbolic of the Archer's Salute. Legend has it that this salute dates back to the English longbowman, who fought the French and once caught, his index and middle-fingers would be chopped off. This led to the practice of the 'archer's hare' being held aloft to show all his fingers were intact, a story allegedly connected with the Battle of Agincourt (1415).

ANTLER MAN - Tom Lock of Hawkridge (b.1926). 3

ARTISTIC FREEDOM 4
In memory of 'V.G' – Viola Gardner (1913-1991) – Artist and eccentric who lived near Brendon, Devon. When asked by the Land Agent how she reached the remote part of the moor, she replied that she used wire-cutters.

BAMFYLDE CLUMP - THE ROUND RING 6
Almost 1,000 ft above sea level, found on the SW edge of Exmoor. The beech trees, planted in the 19th century on an ancient cattle pound and burial site, are in a complete circle and visible from a long way in every direction.

BEAST 7
The 'Exmoor Beast' plagued the moor in 1983. Sheep killings were numerous. The carcases and sightings suggested that the culprit was a big cat such as a puma or panther, but none was found.

BREAK **O** - STONE FRAGMENT 8
'Herepaith' (OE) and 'here-paeth' (Saxon) suggest several possible uses. The 'herepath' literally an army path, was a superior road much used by ordinary travellers and traders.

BURGUNDY CHAPEL 10
Little is known about the medieval Chapel, built on North Hill above Minehead, other than it was in a ruinous state by 1717. Its position on the side of a cliff overhanging the sea, suggests it may have been a votive chapel erected in thanksgiving for escape, possibly on return from an expedition to Burgundy.

CHRISTMAS DAY AT RADDINGTON 12
Dedicated to St. Michael, set on the St. Michael's Way (Cornwall to Norfolk). Formally a pagan site, this 13th century church houses a very old Rood screen with naturalistic foliage carving and also a Green Man boss.

CROSSING-KEEPERS 13
The ancient Exmoor Pony Herd can be traced back 2,000 years and are recognisable by their oaten 'mealy-mouths' and they are sturdy and hardy at 11-12 hands. Ponies on Exmoor are mentioned in the Doomsday Book. In 1818, four-hundred were brought from the Exmoor Forest to Winsford Hill where they still graze today. Current numbers are endangered having fallen to below 500.

CULBONE STONE 14
Stands on Culbone Hill close to an incomplete Stone Row. The 5th-7th century Culbone Stone, 3 ft high, is incised with a wheel cross. This is an early Christian symbol of which the lower right arm extends beyond the circle pointing in the direction of the smallest church in England, dedicated to St Beuno.

FMD IN THE WINGS 20
Farming suffered an outbreak of foot and mouth disease in Spring 2001. Whilst Devon suffered deeply at the time and from the aftermath of MAFF Policy (Defra), Somerset and in particular Exmoor, were restricted more by movement of stock rather than slaughter.

FROM ROBOROUGH CASTLE TO THE HOAR OAK TREE 22
Hoar Oak Tree, the latest successor in a lineage of historic oak trees which marked the boundary dividing the Forest of Exmoor and the commons of Lynton and Brendon. The Hoar Oak Tree is often mentioned in the perambulations of the Forest and the original oak fell around the year 1658.

LYNMOUTH DISASTER 30
In August 1952, the East and West Lyn Rivers rose suddenly and flooded with waters from the Exmoor catchment. Large boulders and rocks were carried in the flow towards the village destroying houses, roads and bridges. Thirty-four people lost their lives.

MOON OVER ST LUKE'S 32
The church was built at Simonsbath in 1856 – after the disafforestation of the Royal Forest of Exmoor in 1819 – becoming an ecclesiastical parish. It is the largest parish in England covering over 20,000 acres. The odour of Ramsons, (hrmsa OE) or Wild Garlic *Allium ursinum,* haunts damper ancient woodlands, hollow lanes and stream-banks.

NEW YEAR 34
The valleys of the Doones are some of the settings in the 17th century romance *Lorna Doone* (1869) by RD Blackmore through whose descriptions of the landscapes and peoples of Exmoor he captured the reader's imagination.

ON DUNKERY BEACON 38
Standing at 1,705 ft, occasionally used for celebratory bonfires, most recently on 4th June 2012 for the Royal Diamond Jubilee of HM Queen Elizabeth II.

POINT OF VIEW - *R ponticum* 41
A species of Rhododendron with proliferate purple flowers that can be seen in woodlands during May and June. The bush, which is being systematically eradicated, has become a host to *Phytophthora ramorum*, a fungus-like pathogen, which affects and kills larch trees in Britain.

QRs - THE COLERIDGE WAY 42
A 36 mile walk from Nether Stowey on the Quantock Hills to Porlock passing Webbers Post. Samuel Taylor Coleridge (1772-1834) was the inspiration, together with the natural landscape,

for The Coleridge Way Project co-ordinated by C Jelley and J Mash. In Spring 2013, First School pupils were inspired to write lines whilst walking the Way - a selection of these have been combined into one poem. QR Apps contain these words in nine images.

QR CODE POEMS - The Coleridge Way 43

QR Codes are a form of digital imaging, a type of matrix barcode. A mobile application or 'App' is designed to be read by smartphones, tablet computers and other mobile devices. The nine QR Apps represent a selection of the lines written along The Coleridge Way, which are placed in this poem.

SNOWDROP VALLEY 46

It is said that, in the 13th century, the monks from Dunster introduced the snowdrop to a part of the Avill Valley, now known as Snowdrop Valley, whilst others believe that the plant is anciently native. The wood where most grow is in the North Hawkwell Wood.

THE BALLAD OF CROYDON HILL 49

Croydon Hill with its ancient tradition of a devilish creature is the setting of a folktale that may have its root in real events. The hill has a reputation for being haunted by unearthly howls and is the site of Bat's Castle.

THE LEK 53

The Lek is the traditional mating ground for the Black Grouse. The all-black male has a lyre-shaped tail that is raised to show white under-feathers when displaying. The female is smaller and brown and known as the Greyhen.

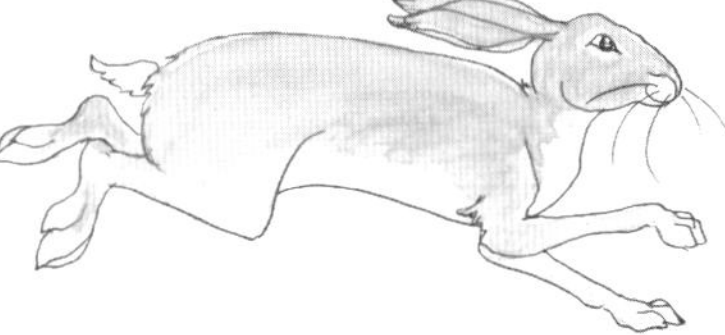

The Editor and Publisher gratefully acknowledges permission to reprint copyright material as follows:

TILLA BRADING - 'Break O - Stone Fragment', previously published as 'Stone Fragment' in Shearsman magazine 2006

ELIZABETH BRADSHAW - 'Christening', won the 2009 Samuel Taylor Coleridge Memorial Poetry Prize under the title 'Winter Christening' and published as such

AUDREY COLDRICK - 'October Air', previously printed in Exmoor Poets by Victor Cloudsdale 2009

SARAH DOYLE - 'The Ballad of Croydon Hill', previously published in The Dawntreader magazine, Issue 019

ATISHA McGREGOR AULD - 'Haiku', previously published in Eight Rivers - A Tributary of Words, by Charmed Hole Publications 2006

FRANCES PRESLEY - 'Bampfylde Clump - The Round Ring', previously published in Osiris 73, 2011

JAY RAMSAY - 'Culbone Stone', previously published in Places of Truth - Journeys into Sacred Wilderness, Awen Publications 2009/2012

RICHARD SPIERS - 'Winter Sky', previously printed in Exmoor Poets by Victor Cloudsdale 2009

ROSEMARY TOEMAN - 'The Heron', previously published in Emptying the Attic, by Jillian Merer and in Above the Marsh and Other Poems by Rosemary Toeman published by John Garland 2007

ANTHONY WATTS - 'Exmoor', received the Samuel Taylor Coleridge Memorial Poetry Prize 2008; later published in Steart Point published by John Garland 2009

ROSINA WINIARSKI - 'November Evening', previously printed in A Pause in Time by Printing at the Vicarage 2013

With special thanks to all those who have contributed to this unique work: to all the poets and to all the individuals listed here in every category and also to those who have supplied general information so freely - including the astronomers, Exmoor Society and Exmoor National Park Authority.

Administration - Elizabeth Colville

Astro Image Adviser - Paul Jeanes

Poetry Co-ordinator and Adviser - Richard Westcott

Proof-reader - Elizabeth Witts

Typesetter - Jane Ruell

Illustrations

Front Cover © David Prentice (b. 1936) 2012
(oil on canvas 16 x 18 inches)
Courtesy © The John Davies Gallery 2013
Moreton-in-Marsh GL56 9NQ

Hares & Green Man © Di Cater 2013

Photograph of Hawthorn Tree © Atisha McGregor Auld 2006

Photograph of Editor with *Dunkery Stag* © Anna Fraser 2013
Courtesy of Dulverton Heritage Centre TA22 9EX

Photo Imaging
© Howard Gimber 2013
Veaseys Printers, Totnes TQ9 5DZ

QR Apps © Christopher Jelley - Storywalks 2013
The Coleridge Way poem compiled by - First Schools:
Dunster, Nether Stowey and Porlock St Dubricus

Astrologue

And behold the height of the stars, how high they are!

Job 22 : 12